The Bir

_by_

Dawn Gorman

First published 2023 by The Hedgehog Poetry Press

Published in the UK by
The Hedgehog Poetry Press
5, Coppack House
Churchill Avenue
Clevedon
BS21 6QW

www.hedgehogpress.co.uk

ISBN: 978-1-913499-67-9

COVER PAINTING
Into the Wild, 2017 by Kate Bergin
Oil on canvas, 70 x 50cm

Contents

'pushed up close'

The Bird Room

There were no birds here,
just books about them,
maps on the walls with a forest of pins
to mark where you'd seen them,
and drawer after drawer of eggs.
My bed was squeezed into a corner.
I drew in my borders so I could fit.
A leopard-print chair
was pushed up close every night
to stop me falling out.
I remember the dusty smell of it,
and beyond, the glint of drawer knobs
I was forbidden to touch.
You'd collected them when it was legal,
took only one from each clutch.
I felt their loneliness,
lifted my face for the same whiff of air.
Sometimes I imagined the unlived chicks
bobbing on perfect, cotton wool sea,
unseen feet kicking at labels.

The Benefit of Distance

Twelve flightless summers then this:
birders' green jackets, tripods
and 'arctic skua' to 'yellowhammer'
on the list in my pocket
waiting to be ticked.
The new binoculars yanked at my neck,
hard circles against my eyes,
a cold smell of metal, men's voices,
all of them waiting to see what I could see.

All I knew was that it was November
and this was a big, grey world.
You pointed out Canada geese
at the far end of the reservoir,
dots that seemed even more remote
as they swam across the trembling glass,
silent as the telly with the sound off.
There was nothing here to hold me.

Decades later, you told me how a man
in Africa looked through your bins
and clapped and laughed at the magic.
Had you hoped for that from me,
or just wanted a point of connection?

Today, while you rest,
I pick them up, that pair
(they seem smaller now),
look through the wide end
and far away can make out
the platinum dance of winter water,
see the benefit of distance,
the way shadow creates light.

Five Forint

If I'd listened to you, read the books
arranged floor-to-ceiling in the bird room,
travelled with you, binoculars ready,
I would know what this bird is,
this slender, long-legged thing, neck folded
back towards its shoulders, long, sharp beak.
I too would quip *great white egret,*
toss the coin on the table,
give a little been-there laugh, say
Kis-Balaton, Coto de Doñana,
I've seen hundreds.

You're forgetting place names now,
have to check those rows of red books,
each a year of birds,
methodical lists in tiny, neat writing,
comments on the cost of everything.

The marshes are forgetting too,
drying out as agriculture and tourism
leach groundwater,
temperatures rise, less rain falls.

But a man you would dismiss
for not being a proper birder
tells me great white egrets
now breed on the Somerset Levels.
I love them for challenging what you knew,
finding their own way to survive.

'this kind of thing'

Ironing Dad's Shirts

She says only bother with the collar and neck
as you wear a jumper over them now,
but time's running out for this kind of thing,
so I press thinned white cotton
like a mother.

You wore them on trips to India
when you strode off to the next bird,
picked your way among snakes in dried-up riverbeds.
Now, your journeys drift like fog from kitchen to lounge.
Draped over dining chairs, shirts quiver, seem to know.

St Edmunds, late August

All the endings begin here.
The limes release a detachment of seeds,
a spin of yellow
to highlight the grass
around Henry Hatcher, historian,
1777–1846, and his unnamed wife.

You used to spin coins on the kitchen table
before I knew about metaphor.
When they slowed, they fell horizontal,
rattled like a fanfare. I liked the alternative
to going round and round.
Now, you fall and fall.

Here, I sit on this bench, watch people
come and go, all the past and future
turning in their heads.
I call to someone's lurcher, stroke its ears,
hear the robin's pebble-on-pebble call,
hold up this fragment of sky with one breath.

Family: Diomedeidae

It was always as if birds came to you by magic
when they appeared on branch, rock, water,
and you exclaimed *I don't believe it!*
then reeled off a name. But of course you believed it –
you'd done your research, knew the jizz backwards.
No question then that it was a black-browed albatross
you spotted from your South African hotel balcony
as it passed, close inshore. In your bird notes,
precisely logged as *Scottburgh, 0700, July 11th 2005,*
you wrote with the excitement of a schoolboy:
From my first sighting, I never saw it flap a wing,
and I watched it out of sight.
You know you are somewhere special
when you get an albatross in the bins.

In your final days, another albatross came,
visible through the hospital window only to you.
Your gaze was steady, sure. Afterwards, in the notes
you'd left in the bird room, addressed to me,
you say in that tiny Parkinson's script
that if you could be any creature, it would be a bird.
I would spread my wings, and go anywhere I wanted.
I sit at your desk with a pile of field guides and read
how seabirds' white undersides can make them difficult
to spot against the sky as they pass overhead.
I will look up then, sometimes, often, imagine
what might be there unseen and think of you,
wings fully extended, wind-shear soaring,
never needing to flap a wing.

'a quiet minute'

My heart is a roomful of birds

They come, feather-close, presenting themselves for inspection – a nuthatch on the path through the woods, a dipper right there on the riverbank, red kite low over the lane – so I don't even need your best binoculars, now on a peg in my hall, just have to be there, and yes, sometimes I get a sense of *wait here and see what happens* – not in my ear, more like the nudge of an invisible shadow – and there it is after a quiet minute or two, a jay's blue flash, some rare jewel, and though I don't count, make lists, I do take note, and realise that they, you, were probably always this close – if only I'd listened, seen, opened the door

'when I remember'

Your Binoculars

I've been using them
for a year now, taking them
to the woods when I remember.
There's still something about their smell
that brings you into focus, but I'll never be able to point
them at a tree and find the right branch, the one with the bird on it.
I did watch two young squirrels through them, they were
chasing each other round an oak tree, then
one time there was a woodpecker on a
trunk right in front of me –
that was much easier.
I'm trying, Dad.

But listen (wherever you are)
I just googled them, Leica 10x42s,
they're worth a fortune. So now
I think of how we balanced them on
your coffin at the crem, imagine
you moaning at us from the ether –
Don't let 'em tumble, they'll never
be rait again if they fall on t' floor.

Let me reassure you then –
I always put the strap around
my neck so I can't drop them (sorry
I was so unfixably clumsy). I know I'll never
lift them to feel the same thrill you had when you spotted
some rare bird, and, let's be honest, I won't ever see things your way
(that was the trouble with us, wasn't it?). But I hope I'll
find that flittering thing I'm looking for. It's
not in the bird books, I know that.
Maybe it was in your heart.
Maybe it's in mine.

Dawn, c.1966

Dawn Gorman is a creative writing tutor and mentor, and works with poetry in therapeutic settings. She is Poetry Editor of *Caduceus* magazine, and presents *The Poetry Place* monthly radio show on West Wilts Radio. She collaborates widely – her work has been turned into a symphony, films, porcelain artworks and dance, and has appeared in journals including *Poetry Ireland Review, Under the Radar, Iota, Magma* and *The Rialto.* Her publications include the Brian Dempsey Award winner *Instead, Let Us Say* (Dempsey & Windle, 2019), and two Pushcart Prize-nominated pamphlets – *This Meeting of Tracks,* published in the four-poet book *Mend & Hone* (Toadlily Press, 2013), and *Aloneness is a Many-Headed Bird* (Hedgehog Poetry Press, 2020), a conversation in poetry with Rosie Jackson.